A FAMILY ALBUM

Poetry by Dan Liberthson

San Francisco, Dan Liberthson, 2006

"Passing On," "In a Catholic Church," and "Mother Loss"
appeared in The Neovictorian/Cochlea.
"Suicide (Aunt Frances)" appeared as "Suicide" in
South Coast Poetry Journal.
"Dad" appeared in Black Buzzard Review.

Cover photo by Kathy Rawlins and Joe Bui

Cover layout by Joe Bui Art Direction
and Fish Tank Maintenance

ISBN-10: 0-9787683-0-2
ISBN-13: 978-0-9787683-0-0

To obtain additional copies of this book, please visit
liberthson.com or any major on-line book vendor.

Printed in the U.S.A.

This book is dedicated to Kathy Rawlins and Judy Windt,
my first wise and patient readers, and to my fellow writers
who helped lick these poems into shape.

Contents

Beginning Matters

This book got its start just after the turn of the millennium, and not long after I turned 50. On a rainy January weekend, I found myself cleaning out closets in an attempt to sort the clutter of years. In a worn cardboard box unopened through many moves were three battered photo albums I had forgotten existed. That evening, neck stiff after hours poring over these fragments of my life, I felt that I had to give them and those they survived the attention deserved after long neglect, and tell the story of the labyrinth that was my family.

The neglect was earned, because this was not a happy family history, but a broken one that I struggled to escape throughout a prolonged adolescence and a difficult early adulthood. Yet it was a history that, from a relatively safe distance, I could re-live in the light of survival, not the dark of the conflict. This was a story of would-be loving parents defeated by the mental illness of my gifted, beautiful younger sister, with whom neither, though both professional healers, could cope. It was the story of her ongoing ordeal, and of the tortured confusion of my own feelings for and against her, which forced me both to reject her completely and to try to *be* her, by becoming as ill as she was. It was the story of my fun-loving, much older half-sister, resentfully stuck with us all, and of the extended family who paraded across the stage of our tragedy every few years. Yes, it was a tragedy, but one, like many others, with lightning moments of brightness that also demand recognition.

This book is not in chronological order, and although the poems are in part grouped by family member, they are mainly arranged by theme. Some of these themes are cultural, and relate to the American immigrant experience of my parents and grandparents, as well as the impact that formative experience had on the second generation— my own. In many poems, the story line and logic are straightforward, but in some, particularly in the central series about my damaged sister, I convey extreme stress and mental schism by warping both story and sense. In poems like these, the reader's main reward may be in empathizing with the distressed characters, rather than trying to untangle every twist in logic.

Please rely for additional meaning on the photographs that stimulated many of the poems, and on the labyrinth patterns that precede and echo the photos. At first, to allow readers to imagine and relate to their own versions of the people in the poems, I intended to leave out the photos, but they began to insist, so in they went. I hope that, as you read this book, you won't limit yourself by labeling the photos or the poems as *only* mine, but will relate to them as common human experience, and be rewarded with empathy for and insights into people in your own life.

Dan Liberthson, 2006

Dad and I in Black and White

You sit in a wicker rocking chair, my dad,
in three-piece suit and windsor-knotted tie
and hold me on your shoulder, high,
my infant body molding to your face.
We smile, yours stiffer than mine,
alike in stuck-out ears but more
in joint elation, side by side.

Behind, a window melts in sun so bright
the camera's shocked eye blazes white.
The chair is white, your shirt, the radiator too,
my diaper and the photo's edge.
All this brightness buoys our image
in the camera's life-preserving ring.
Beneath, a dark river runs.

This was before it all went wrong
and we became adversaries,
rams butting heads for the life
you wanted back and I refused to give.
Joy leached from smiles
stretched as in hard exercise.

My appetite grew as yours shrank,

a loss you hid until cancer

sniffing along your dwindling spoor

caught you and ate away your meat

to show the heavy bones

bluewhite beneath waxpaper skin.

Outside the hospital window

beyond fluorescent glare

a hard October rain falls, and night.

A few late leaves

cling to the lawn.

What's left?

Ashes

and through the lens

smiles.

The dark river passing through.

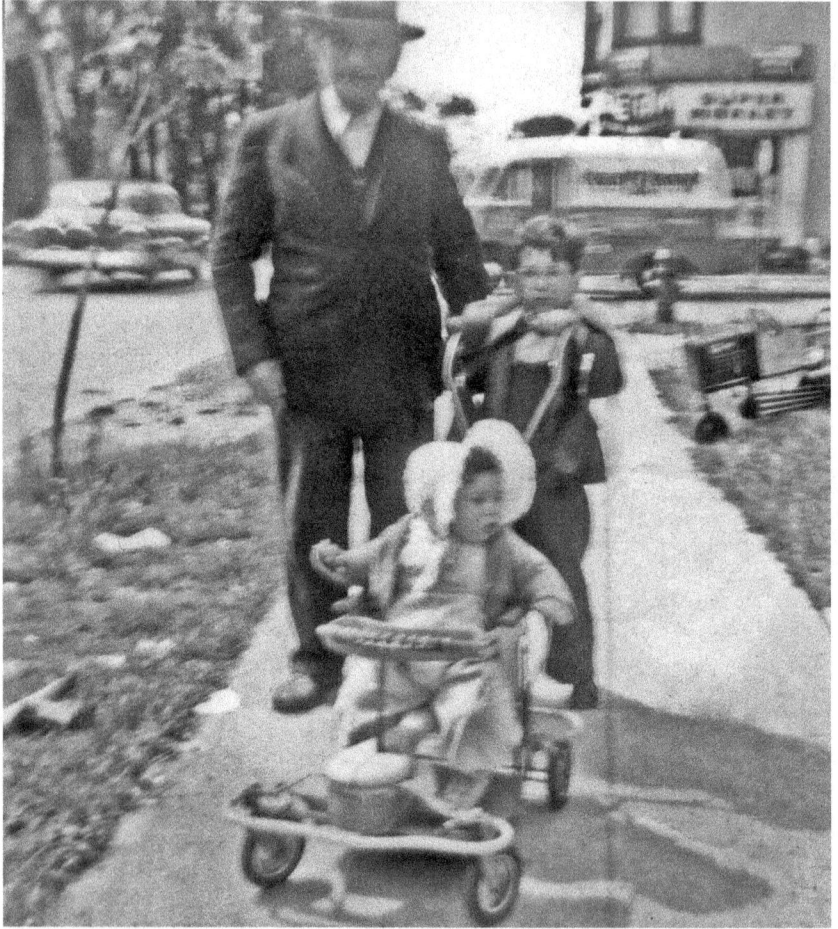

Two Early Photos

In the first,
I push you, little sister,
in your buggy,
sunhat flapped back,
all in whites.
I am in darks,
grim with responsibility
while you are beating
the buggy-front baby style but
unsmiling, looking left at something
terribly exciting—or scary.
Behind, a guiding or restraining hand
at my shoulder, Zeydeh, also dark
except for his white fedora,
stiff and toothless, creaks along.

It is Spring: a few spots of dirty snow
stain worn-out grass.
Behind us, a domed white delivery van,
its sign unreadable, speeds

past the "Peak" market fifty years ago:
the truck recycled many times since,
like the snow, the grass, the market,
the old man gone after his teeth.

The future that so alarmed you
is here. Your fear was justified,
but so was your excitement,
for as this future too speeds past,
whatever waits, we go on.

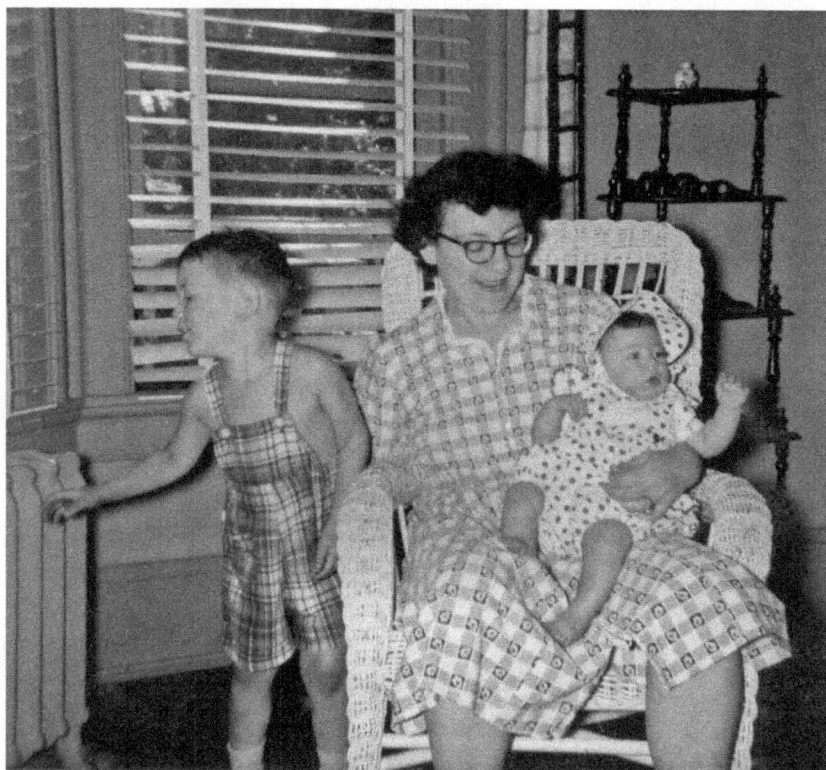

2

In the second,

I stand to one side of Mother

who sits in the wicker chair.

I am reaching right, distracted,

in a plaid jumpsuit,

and she wears checks too

but her attention goes the other way,

toward you flapping on her lap, reaching

left for something else out of view.

Her hand, large and white

against your polkadot frock,

passively restrains but does not hold,

just as, when I was hurt

and came for comfort, she would

put her arms around me if pressed

but leave them resting there

like inert sea animals.

Even as a child I felt

you and I were impositions

on her private time,

loved in principle but not with heart,
as though she were a mother
with no call to mothering.

Perhaps that's why
in this picture we look away
from her and from each other—
no common love draws us close.
That's how we grew, facing away,
each embraced by solitude,
waiting for her to hold us.

Passing On

1

Father of my name and dreams,
your shadow moves over my blood.
Like a candleflame your death
burns in the dark of my bones.

From the black anvil of Diaspora,
forged and tempered with grief,
you lifted the riches of poverty,
a pedlar's bitter treasure.

Your father, a pedlar before you,
walked clear over the cold Atlantic
straight from the Ukraine to New York
shouldering his Chagallian sack.

Liberty would not bend her neck
and he could never unbend his,
so he trudged unfreed to the Bronx
and passed on his burden to you.

2

I believe you tried to ditch that sack.
I see you draw it back, like a hammer thrower,
but it's too heavy and you topple over.
Crushed beneath it, you decide:

Who in the New World would buy
this age-old bag of miseries?
It's yours for keeps: you open it
and don the armor stashed inside.

With liberty at last, but monumental—
armor grand and glittering by my time—
you see no more than what your visor shows:
a vision that can pierce but not embrace.

Light enough for the Macabees,
it staggers you but bears you up:
you earn an M.D., raise it for a shield,
and never leave yourself unarmed again.

3

When I unmade the family exodus,
flying East for freedom,
crossing to the Old Country I saw
your father's bootprints in the water.

You did not chase your prodigal—
I'd never escape, you knew,
because I'd never really left:
Masada is not large, but everywhere.

So when your loneliness demanded
I left the dream of exile and came home:
you smiled and raised your shield
and made your love known:

Dark and hard, a guard
against easy comfort and false hopes.
You wanted us to stand together,
protectors of the bitter treasure.

4

But I wore no armor
and yours would not come off,
so each stood alone as the years passed:
I, the squire, whose service was to witness,

and you, half dragon, half knight
jousting with yourself as I looked on,
corrosion spreading from your bitter core.
No surgery could free you when you fell:

you had become the armor you once wore,
hollow at the last, a clapperless bell—
your silence was so loud,
my head rings still.

When the final fire burned down
and the quick of you melted into me,
we were one at last, and I was warmed
until the bronze cooled again and cast.

Now my heart too is hollow,
my sunsets cold beyond measure.
Distant is the song of the birds
but mine, all mine, is the treasure.

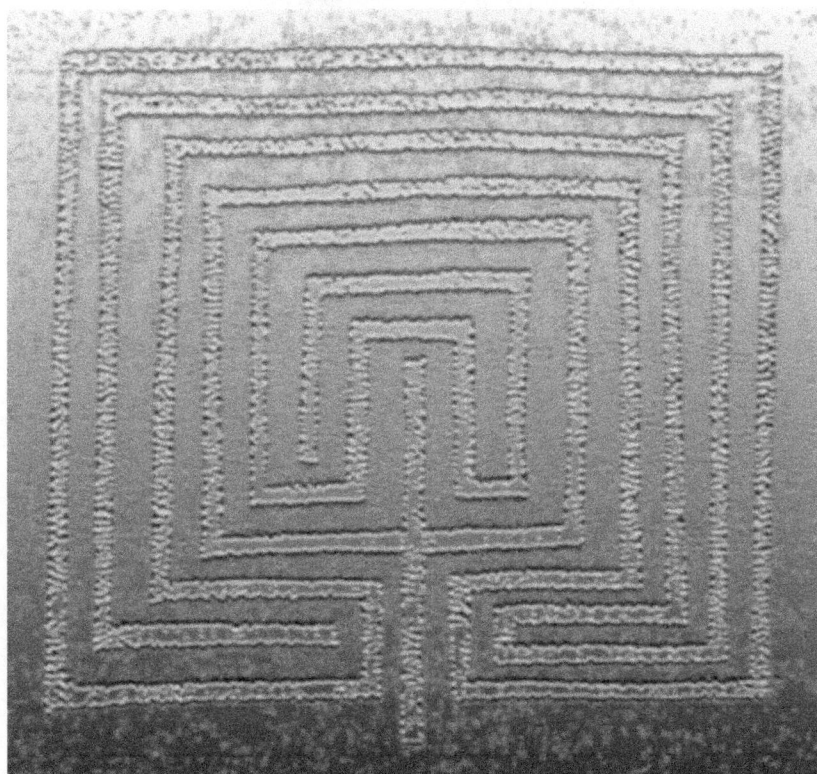

Flying to Europe I Visit
Great-Aunt Anna in New York

I'd never seen anyone so old!
Arms thin as broomsticks:
the left, broken on the ship from Russia,
healed inches short and nourished
the bitterness of her life
that filled her and left her empty.

"She was beautiful," Mother said,
"skin like milk, hair like fire—
spirit, and such intellect!
But she frightened men,
took their attention for pity,
and never trusted a one."

Aunt Anna's mind,
dried brittle like her body,
glinted behind skin
roughened by ten thousand weathers:
shapes moved there, lonely
but unreachable.

She couldn't believe
I could carry three bags of groceries
stacked in her pushcart
two blocks down the sidewalk
and up four flights to that gritty apartment
acrid with the smell of her.

I was too young for her to fathom,
some sort of demigod
admired yet resented,
come to stay and then leave,
flaunting the careless strength
of an eighteen-year-old.

"It's good you are strong, Danny,
but you should learn to be careful
or life will get you! Hold back
a little or one day you'll break something,
or something will break you." I snorted,
immortal in second-generation skin

thickened with the bricks
of my parents' labor.
I had no idea how large was this ocean
she had crawled and I would fly across,
how unforgiving of misstep, and cold,
a mockery of young hope

so intolerant of restraint.
She knew and I knew this sudden,
self-serving visit was my last, our last,
but she wished me good voyage,
narrowed her eyes, tilted her head,
took my hand in her knuckly ones.

"I was young once, and I
crossed the Atlantic, just like you,
but it's not what you think,
either here or there. Be careful
of Europe! You can't trust it—
if at first you are impressed

by the beautiful things there,
think how many people
died to make or take that beauty.
Come back where it's safe:
study medicine, that would be wise,
not running here, running there."

I embraced her very gently,
not to crack this sapless tree,
but feeling her hollow bones
echo so close, warning
of what I would be, shuddered.
She felt it and turned away.

"It's never what you think.
You leave this place, come to that,
promises made are promises broken,
and you learn the truth from lies.
It's the same there or here:
nobody stays—they come, they go."

Puppy Love

I truly loved Aunt Marion,
a tender soul who put on
toughness as she needed
to work with delinquents,
to whose glory I aspired,
who always knew
when I cheated at canasta
and did me one better,
whose horsy face
with large bright yellow teeth
and eyes jaundiced by hepatitis
were so lovely ugly
they charmed everyone,
even sullen me when
she'd toss her head,
grin spinster great with joy of simply living
and neigh her laughter, loud and pure.

I was so proud to be hers,
that she would play
with this pimply juvie wannabe,

Charles Atlas in his sock drawer,
posing for the mirror every day,
waiting for his biceps
to bear the promised fruit,
imagining his jackknife a switchblade,
oh so tough, though Marion knew
(and did I care?) that he was really,
like her, a cream-puff.

Aunt Marion flicked out cards
deftly with long fingers
yellow in their nailbeds like
pieces of sun, but her wrist
showed moon-white when she drew.
Tendons strung only for me to see,
she'd slip the new card slyly
into her back-tipped fan,
smiling as if it were an ace,
not a deuce,
and let me drag on her cigarette,
holding her hand along my cheek

in a practical caress, ready to snatch it away

(*your mother will kill me, sweetie!*)

as I grabbed with my lips, my teeth,

and she giggled as we alone

outfoxed the family-heavy world,

until she reached over and tickled

my ribs, and I opened, gasping

and choking, and there she sat—

blowing smoke rings and grinning.

Jesus I loved you, Marion.

Oh my sweet Aunt Marion,

why did you have to die

and leave me here

to draw my cards all alone?

Dad as Polyphemus

You crack
in thick bare hands
walnuts, crushing one
against its brother.
Sad wrinkled brains
break from their skulls.
Jauntily, you toss them
into your upturned mouth,
grind their sweet flesh
despite the tiny screams
you *must* hear,
grind them with teeth
caged in glass all night
like wild dogs, raging at me
in a silent, savage dream.

You swallow, smile,
and hold one out to me.

A Dream of Salt Water

Dismasted,
toy of the waves,
I bob and rock
wherever the storm beats.

The clouds pulse,
salt-heavy rain
drags me down
into wave pits.

I am not Odysseus,
blessed, as I'd hoped,
with a goddess
to bring me ashore,
but lightning bait,
to freeze and burn.

I am faithless,
cherish vengeance,
glittering idols
and false coin—
against orders
of the Jealous God.

Dare I ask forgiveness?

The one who never forgets
shakes his trident and laughs.
The one who could forgive
will arrive too late.
The one to whom I was born
turns his back
and walks beyond the horizon
as the salt water
closes in.

Dad Tells All

When you told me
many years into my twenties
that you'd had women
other than my mother
whenever you could manage
without risk of discovery
in your apparent marriage
I wondered why, now,
you told me, and whether
somewhere was another me

living unmolested
by the feeling, deep as touch,
that something was wrong,
had always been wrong—
a happier me
not needing always
to keep his eye on the ball,
only to live, with no sense
that any lapse of concentration
would let the world fall apart.

"The women meant nothing, only
a good time, and I deserved that much
especially after your sister went nuts.
Life was hard, pure suffering.
Your mother was wonderful,
tried like hell and never stopped, but
she had all kinds of hang-ups. You know
she'd never let me go down on her?
Thought it was dirty. Anyway,
what she didn't know couldn't hurt."

You expected my approval
but I was away, reliving
one chilly Fall day in childhood:
kept outdoors, I replayed the World Series
against your office wall
with a worn-out tennis ball
and in the end
Mantle off Koufax put it through
the green-painted window again.
You were much angrier than usual.

And when I came back,
you were telling me, smiling,
how much fun you
and Mrs. Lukatch had
on the stirupped exam table
in your office behind that
green-painted window,
a doctor playing doctor—
and I wondered *why now*,
felt stunned green inside

and found myself on the lawn
chasing down flyballs you threw
carefully just beyond my reach
the few times I got you to play—
made again the impossible
shoestring catch of twenty years ago,
looked up with grass-stained grin to hear
"the best players make the hard plays
look easy, son, but you
make the easy plays look hard."

And when I came back,

there you were, old man

worshipping yourself

young and unaccountable,

asking me to understand, no, *admire*

ancient conquests that meant nothing

when all that meant anything

lay in green shards on the ground

slicing me like raw meat as I dove

for your last uncatchable throw.

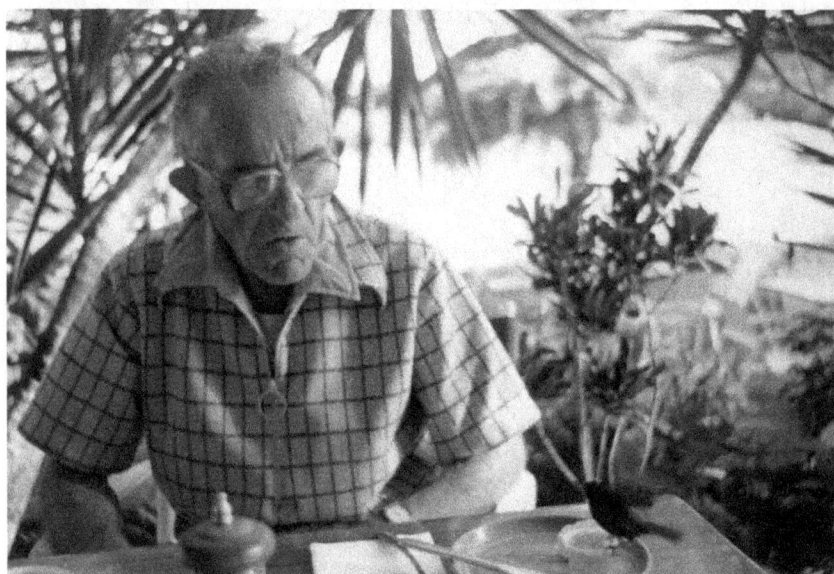

Dad's Death

1

When the agonal breaths had stopped
with a last sigh
as your lungs gave up
and a tear rolled down your cheek
leaving a trail slick as a snail's—
I did something I'd never have dared
while you lived. I put my thumb
gently on one eyelid, my middle finger
on the other, as if playing
a soft minor chord.
I wanted to see if any life was left:
thought or vision unsaid
(for there'd been no closing words)
that I could read with fingertips
like Braille. But you were gone, Dad.

Neither of us ever believed
in anything but our lives
and I, shadowed by your myth,
often barely that. But now,

feeling those cool, tough orbs

lack the least flutter,

I needed some sign

and closed my own eyes

the better to see

where you might be.

2

In Guadeloupe, our last trip,

you were worn out after we'd driven

and fought all day. We argued

from habit and for sport

but on that trip no longer could

pretend the game was fun.

Like rival caged birds,

we had at last drawn blood.

At sundown we sat

across a cafe table

and I could see your toughness

had worn thin and brittle,

hollow stalk waiting for the wind.

A small black sparrow perched warily
on your plate and begged for crumbs.
You tried to whistle but only blew,
a low, failing breeze. The bird flew
and your head slowly turned to follow,
barely keeping pace, eyes large
and pale blue behind thick lenses.
In that instant I first knew
you were going, you would be gone.

And I wanted to say
tell me Dad, now before you go
who you are, who you think I might be.
But I had never said anything like that
and how could I say it now?
The sparrow flew back as you studied
an old dog dozing in shade.
The bird cheeped and you shifted your gaze,
smiling a bit, and pushed him a crumb.

3

Your eyes still told nothing
except that you were gone.
I stroked your cheek
and felt the wet of a tear.
As I turned away, it told
your last message:
something I could feel,
not hear.

I brought my fingers
to my tongue
and tasted salt,
yours and mine.

Dad Eats a Hardboiled Egg

He cradles it with thick fingers egg-cup shaped,
admires it for a long moment, pale blue eyes
struggling for focus behind thick lenses,
turns it carefully counterclockwise, passing
its seemingly uniform surface before his gaze
as though he alone can see difference there,
a range of snowy mountains and fertile valleys
in this perhaps the only egg left, a world
within a world bereft. His orbit around the egg
now complete, he steadies and carefully
starts to crack it, turning the oval
and rapping it deftly on the table edge
at regular mathematical intervals
he of all his family has discovered
or had passed down to him
by his parents' parents and beyond.
Appraising the web of cracks, he nods
as though he and his egg have found
the answer to a tough question,
the key that fits the lock of the door
to the future. Now he disrobes the egg,

studiously peeling it naked, stroking clean

of shell shards the smooth uncovering skin

with his tobacco-stained fingers,

careful not to blemish the white sheen.

Lips slightly parted, tongue touching their curves,

breathing slow and shallow, he appreciates

the full being of the egg, ovoid promise

of a small pleasure he learned to cherish

through hungry years on the Lower East Side,

of which he said *the only blessing was learning*

to enjoy the simplest things. Now he may be thinking,

two of these end to end make infinity, but I am happy

with this finite joy, this single egg.

Then those blunt strong fingers shape themselves

around the tapered hexagonal salt shaker

with its familiar dented metal head,

and the right hand lifts it toward the left.

His startlingly sharp tongue

snakes out as he bows his head to lick the left hand

(firmly holding the egg in its fist) at the cleft

between the thumb and index finger.
He raises his head and shakes an exact measure
of salt onto the wet spot as if ending a ritual dance.
Again he pauses, solemn, expectant gaze
worshipping the unspoiled surface, and in
the unifying silence of that moment
I recall him saying, before the meal began,
All work is sacred, even menial labor,
and the reward of a job well done
is to eat your food with peace in your heart,
knowing you are entitled.

Dad sighs, *ahhhhh,*
lightly smacks his lips, raises his hand
to lick the salt and then at last
bites through the wall of the chamber of paradise
clear to the yellow sun within, with such a light of joy
spilling from his eyes that even twelve years gone
it warms me still.

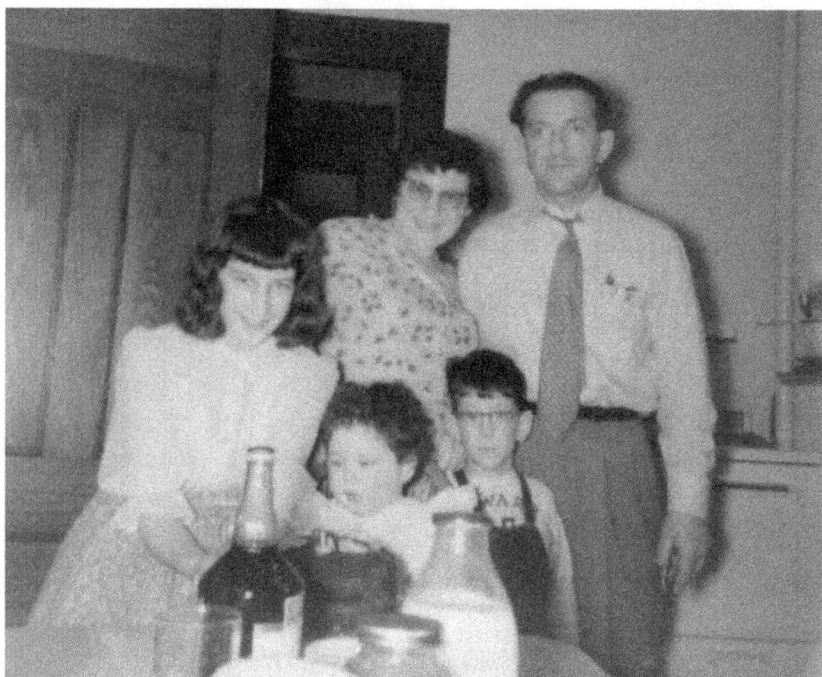

Potato Latkes in Winter:
a Medieval Cast of Mind

Such hubbub in the kitchen:

locating the grinder parts,

getting out the pan,

finding the peanut oil—

there's no sour cream?

Damn! Then applesauce

will have to do, Mother says—

and she will peel and Judy

set the grinder up (she's so mechanical!)

and Danny turn the S-curved crank:

he has energy to burn and loves

the crunch of crisp white meat,

to see potato grind and surge

and drop from the holes

like icicles melting in the sun

and falling into snow. He loves

the oniony smell as Mother

fries and flips and glides each latke

from her spatula
to the brown paper bag to drain,

loves this rare taste of family,
good and thick like applesauce,
as everyone busies about, too bent on flavor
to argue and upbraid, to tear
the daily wounds we always trade.

But he doesn't love it when, slyly,
those white braids turn into maggots
like the ones he saw in yesterday's garbage,
but longer and more numerous,
wiggling down to a porridge of dead matter.

Doesn't love, but knows already, ten years old,
how to read this sign of what the future holds:
this brief grace, thimbleful of time, will grind
in tomorrow's blades, soil that nourishes will
corrode, everything warm will end up cold;

yet senses too that this warm wind

easing through a crack in winter

will return when needed most, expected least,

in a time of desolation,

the rare embracing scent of family

rising again.

A Fairy Tale

I'll tell you a fairy tale.
Once there was a girl,
green-eyed, lithe and blond—
or were they hazel eyes?
No matter:
she was the slim only
beauty in a squat ugly world,
that's what counts.

She was wounded.
Oh, she was stabbed
by a wild unicorn, milkwhite
and beautiful as she.
No, that's not right—
unicorns don't violate,
do they?
Unicorns *are* violated.

Then *she* was the unicorn?
for in a fairy tale

there must be a unicorn, yes?

Maybe *I* was the unicorn,

gone mad because dazed

by auburn beauty,

milk-white, hazel-eyed?

No, not I, but surely someone

simply mutilated her brain.

And it was worse than sadness

worse than death or blindness—

all warped rotten, the beauty,

funhouse-mirrored to bizarre and

barren (say it!) *madness* or

shall we use the clinical pejorative

schizophrenia?

Oh dear! I promised you a fairy tale

but this has gotten real.

I'm sorry. I can't help it.

I'm weeping blood, you see.

But it's OK—
There's still magic!
I can't tell
if the blood's from *her* or *me*!

There! Now we're certain
none of this is real,
it *is* a fairy tale, and so the
unicorn is neither her nor me but
some spiteful poltergeist
sent by ever-loving G-d to teach
arcane lessons in grin-and-bear-it or
this is your life, lump it or deal it—

But what about *her* life you
asshole Deity, what the fuck
were you trying to prove?
That in your wondrous wisdom
you could crap up the most beautiful
green-eyed, chestnut-haired
princess and change her into
a gimp-minded twist toad?

Oh dear, I've screwed up again.
Betrayed the fairy tale.
But please believe me—
if we all just keep the faith,
accept the lot, love everyone,
all will come right in the end.
Right in our end, that is,
rammed in by yours truly G-d—

Stop it! The unicorn is trembling
in the woods, where someone hacked
off his horn and poked out his eyes and
he wanders making little blistered
unicorn noises like in cartoons
oooh, auugh, wheoo, gaaraack, awwwk
but we are all laughing
so it can't be real.

All this apparent blood coursing down
his (or her?) hide, every side runneled
with gore, must be catsup, yes?
Then it really *is* a fairy tale

and soon everything will get better:

The unicorn will heave a sigh

and spring to its feet laughing

and gentle rain will wash away the blood

and from the ground where red rivers run

will spring crimson flowers.

Just as in myth it will happen:

therapy will work, the drugs take effect,

the unicorn eat the flowers and never

die and always love everywhere reign, amen—

but wait just a goddamned minute.

I'm getting hysterical because unicorns

never laugh—*but this one did*—which means

the fairy tale's a fake and somebody

really stole my beautiful sister and

I couldn't pay the ransom so they broke

her brain into a bowl and scrambled it

and now she can't speak straight and her green

fuck hazel eyes are turned inside-out and—

Who kidnapped my sister's brain?

Sir, please control yourself!

We're sorry our officers couldn't find

those bad men in time but of course

you failed to pay

a perfectly reasonable ransom

and the truth is

our utmost efforts couldn't have saved her.

But the best news is

they fried it but they never

ate it! We caught them

red-handed or you might say

open-mouthed hah hah and so

it is our sincere pleasure to offer

a token of our esteem:

Is this the brain, Sir,

you reported missing?

Oh and by the way—

they said they were working for you.

How You Got This Way and What Now

It started when we were kids, the night
the Zeydeh died of a heart attack. He
slipped down into tepid bath water
and was gone. Nobody knew
until the next day except you.
As the storm came in, we made

scary finger shadows with a flashlight
on my bedroom wall, and even when
thunder broke and lightning shocked,
you kept giggling until suddenly
all went quiet and I whispered
"Boy, this is weird!" You looked down

and began to sob as if you were lost
at just the time he must have died.
The air swelled and paused and bled.
You felt him pass like a waning wind,
then turned, walked to the corner
by my Roy Rogers lamp, and gently

lay your face against the wall.

You were never the same again.

Later, I got the idea some hooked shard

of that bitter old man, who chose to love you

instead of me, caught your life in passing,

tore away part and muddled the rest.

Much later, I learned it was a smothering

breach birth and melting chicken-pox fever

that fused and re-fused your brain.

"One insult, it's tolerable," the shrink said, "but two?

You can't compensate. Buoyancy goes

and in comes brain damage."

Imagine it: dry rot, cracking plaster, peeling paint.

Sing it: O-C-D, A-D-D, M-O-U-S-E.

Define it: obsessive, depressive, regressive—

so many names for one result: loneliness.

Your spirit tries to live despite your broken brain,

like a gas-starved engine on a fractured chassis

running on fumes, shaking itself apart.
Fifty years ago you first went missing,
four-year-old quarry of a family hunt
that raged through glass-strewn alleys
and caught you staring into the grease pit
at Beggy's corner gas station.

"I'm gonna get Zeydeh back," you whisper—
"he's in that big hole
just like Mommy said."
You strain toward the pit
as Mother pulls you back,
but slipping your mitten

stand still for a second
shocked by freedom, then
start to scream and stamp,
a strange tarantella of grief
for everything taken away
that will never come back.

On the lot was a wrecked convertible:
"Wrapped it 'round a phone pole,"
Beggy said, and the pole's ghost
still grooved the red driver's door.
"Just like James Dean," Mother sighed:
"such a terrible waste of talent."

"Hunnerd-twunny mile an hour when he hit!"
Beggy whistled. "There weren't much left to bury
I'll bet." You pulled away again, ran,
and fit yourself neatly into the car's groove.
Mother gasped and yanked you out
but your eyes pulled back there all the way home.

That was one of many lost times,
like pages torn from the book of your life:
twelve years gone into a bottle of Mellaril
when you were little more than a sponge
soaking and releasing unconscious blood
and the few slow thoughts and labored words

buoyant enough to break the drug's gravity.
When you emerged from that drowning cave,
hauled toward the surface by some last
lungful of life that refused more such *treatment*,
you came out blinking in sunlight and full of
wonder at the brain you found still sparking

after the long deep of years, a Rip Van Winkle
stunned with all the change: our parents dead
like theirs, and you grown wide and me gray
but still here, both, listening for the promise
of repair, some new drug or miracle that might
leave you whole and sound on the same beach

where breakers smashed you long ago.
Meanwhile, storms arrive and pass,
sunlight and shadow play in the trees
and we ache with their beauty and our loss
but still invite the next day in,
watch the leaves change, fall, and grow again.

A Real Man

"A real man accepts responsibility."
You said that, Mother.
"No matter how far you run
you can't get away from yourself."
You were quoting Alfred Hitchcock,
some film about evil redeemed by good.
So strongly did I need to run from you
and stay, I had no choice but split in two.

I'm only going to say this once.
Put down my sister's head,
Dr. Frankenstein, and go to your room.
And I mean now.
I accept responsibility.
If you think for one minute this movie
has a monster other than me,
you'd better think again.

I admit I broke my sister, *and* I'll fix her.
Saved her dolls, didn't I?

Damn, I'm a better surgeon than you!
Legs to trunk, head to torso, hands to arms,
I've done them all—ripped them off first, true,
but only to advance science
and her moral education.
She had to learn not to cry:

that even the apple of her eye,
the Raggedy Ann she loved more than me,
drawn and quartered by the Official Torturer,
could be healed. I fixed her, Dr. Frank,
and the scar is only just visible
if you open the blouse and look
if you open the mind and look.
She had to learn

not to flinch when the steel went in,
when sweet dreams were sectioned out
and nightmares transplanted from a dead
brain, compliments of the Queen of Night
for whom torment is delight.

She had to learn to love her hated life.
You worked with levers and lightning,
Dr. Frank—I, with my sinister surgical self.

You see, I learned responsibility,
developed a parallel gift for madness,
tried it in various styles and seasons,
taught myself just how it feels
never to know where the monster hides,
from what angle the blow will come
but always, cunning sure,
that it *will* come.

You're free to go now, Dr. Frank.
Your punishment's up—
it's time for mine.
Go back to the village,
welcome your obscurity.
I'll carry on the work
in the glare of the flames, the spotlight
where our monster lives, in pain.

What I can't fix I can't run from,

what I can run from I can fix.

It's the paradox every great surgeon faces.

So I'll crawl the rubbled floor and feel

for missing pieces as the fire takes hold,

wipe them off and try my best to fit,

like pieces from mixed jigsaw puzzles,

the fragments of our lives, our brains.

Sister, We Meet Again

In Mount Hope Cemetery, Rochester, New York
we sat one long November hour, late afternoon,
on a low brown bench under a pale blue sky
and spoke of living among the dead.

It was our first time together
in more than ten years, since
I had left you in your illness
to our father's care, now dead.

Your descent was more than he could take.
Patience was never his, and rage tore up
whatever love dared and made his care all misery,
for he was tied too tight in the knot of you.

He went out nearly eaten away, bitter
from struggle against a bond he could neither
break nor bear, grateful for freedom at last,
unbound from all sharp wishes and remorse.

It passed to me, the duty and the dread,
the love buried deep as the dead,
the hope and despair of finding who
lived weighted down beneath your skin.

You moved and spoke as though
under water, brain pudding thick
with Mellaril, yet there was slow
rhyme in your words, unknowing

grace in your gestures, shed and
left behind like a cape thoughtlessly
cast off by a dancer once high on the stage,
now old, undressed and led to bed.

It seemed that in that slow hour
the dead did not drag at us,
hungry and lonely
in their habitual hopelessness,

but pushed us away, out, up,
as if their dissolving bodies
that powered the trees into the sky
fueled us two alive, you and I,

to host the breath they no longer
could take, to feel whatever joy
or sorrow they had left behind,
whatever bright stirrings of mind

now in their clay-packed dwellings
they scarcely sensed a shadow of.
Only a vast wordless knowing
filled their spaces: that no one should be dead

in life, sealed off by voices and the drugs
it takes to still them, or shut away by rage
at all that ruined your beauty and your wit,
and left you slumped on this low bench.

No one should be dead who still

holds air, the same through which all

starlings hurl and squirrels vault.

Time enough for that, long time enough.

It was deep Fall and all the leaves

curled, sucked dry and crunching

like breaking bone.

But we and the dead sensed Spring

growing green, poised to well through

the brown cold with the ground's strength

to break its own hold and lift high, cast wide,

astonished in July like a sunflower's eye.

And in that place of death I knew

you would soon come back to living,

and I would find my life too,

our voices singing out in a world

solid as the battered wood of our bench

or the gray, attending gravestones

standing to present the dear

departed past to the wanting future.

I was not surprised then

when you said as we stood to go,

"I'll stop taking it in Spring because

I want to *see* the flowers, you know?"

I took your hand only in my mind

because real touch would have frightened

you (and me), and we left together more alive

for the dead, brother and sister, leading, led.

We Visit Niagara Falls, Maddest Sister, and the Devil Too

So far from home you were afraid

to let me out of your sight, afraid

I would leave you lost

in the warm spring sun

you couldn't feel for the cold

fear gripping.

Afraid that Immigration

would put you in jail

in darkest Canada for life

because you heard your Devil,

whom you'd called before you knew it,

curse that bored but pleasant

roundfaced Customs man

and you thought you'd done him

some terrible harm. But you walked on,

with me, over the Rainbow Bridge,

able to brave it only because of me,

though frightened I was the very Devil

you'd heard, you always heard.

The sky went on sunning and bluing
as the mist of the Falls flew over us
and look! You could see rainbows,
so many rainbows! How could that Devil
hide among colors so glorious?
But there He was, behind the elm,
near the rail, pointing his tail,
whispering, *over. Over!*

"Don't go so close to the edge,"
you cried, "You could fall, I could
make you even if I don't want to.
He might make me." And I watched
that horrendous fat trunk of water
in huge slowmotion gouts plunge
down and down and down again
and felt it all fall through me,
tear me loose from myself
and from the wild voice of you,
holding out your arms and backing slowly,
eyes shot wide like prey.

I saw what you were seeing: my body

gouged free, tumbling into the gorge

like a rock torn away, no longer obliged

to hang on, promised deep, sweet oblivion.

He smiled and (this time) that was His mistake.

Something pulled me back. Standing by the elm,

clutching yourself with both arms,

you never could have moved so fast.

Who then or what in the vast world

had saved me? I didn't know

and you were rocking to and fro

like a canary on a swing, thinking

some unfathomable thing.

The world and all its creatures rose up

and rose up again like a giant shuddering

balloon, as desperate to find the sky

as all that weight of water was to fall,

and my tethered body wept to follow.

But I stayed, to wonder whose fear,
yours or mine, might be love in another
guise, the trick of life's trapjaw grip,
clasping us to itself to eat alive,
making gain from our held-fast pain.
The rainbow world still promised
the old future, the lie we could see through:
my deluge done, be fruitful and multiply
for I am thy shepherd. Why then this roar,
these water-wolves, this Devil-blessed descent?

We walked the bridge toward home,
another country where world and mind
deviously change place, and every sight
in every moment's full and dying life
is Devil or Angel, down or up, never level,
but at this moment, held midway between
the river and the sky, it mattered only that we
each had crossed the border and come back:
you and I had traded shores this once,
and now, we faced the sky and smiled.

Leaves

We crested one of the rolling hills
in New York State's Southern Tier,
and the red gold orange fiery glory
burst from its ice-blue frame of autumn sky.

The scent of burning leaves the sharp
thick sweet sour smell of soil the craze
of ever shifting color brought back earliest
crawling memories from before I went West.

I drove in a time-trance, drawn out, down,
into the land I'd rolled on as a child,
torn by the pull of humus smelling
of the death I'd left behind to wait

years ago, the lost life that would never feel
so mud-dark deep in bright California.
I had soul rot, infected by my abandoned youth
treacherously buried in this alluring loam.

Oh a willow! you shouted, pointing,
gasping with grace borrowed from its beauty.
That was Mother's favorite,
so lovely, long and slender, look!

And my skull contorted in steel rings—
because you had remembered and brought alive
the woman who gave me life
and I had forgotten her favorite tree.

You, who not a minute before had been
driving me crazy with paranoid stuff:
Are you sure you won't hit me on the head
and leave me in the woods?

You could murder me
and nobody would know. I thought
don't tempt me I said how can you talk such
drivel! You said you don't understand,

it's my illness. How can you know it's only
your illness but *not* know how crazy it sounds?
It doesn't *feel* crazy, you said. It feels true. You
could be the Devil. The Bible says. But logic

says I'm not, right? Maybe. And I thought how like Mother
you are in voice and gesture, joys and griefs
and even superstitions, in all but her I-beam logic
somehow broken off in you. I sat in the rental car

beside a damaged ghost, born-again spirit split
by a cracked mirror. Oh the colors, you shouted, pointing
and clapping your hand to your chest as she always did.
Look at the colors! I drove on into a blurring red sea.

Seeing the Leaves

Good, better, best
never let it rest
until the good is better
and the better, best.

You would recite that ditty,
Mother, nodding with the rhythm,
wearing a pacified grin, in times
of doubt or hesitation, like a rosary,
whenever you needed comfort.

Each Fall on a carefully calculated day,
you would gather us into the car
and we'd start, always later than planned,
on the three-hour drive southeast to Naples
to see the leaves.

Each year they were not quite as *good*
as last year or three years ago, always
not quite as good, fated to go *down-hill*
as restaurants inevitably did and City
services or anything you could name.

Did you ever ask, what is a *good* leaf
and what is a *bad* leaf? Did you ever
stop the car, get out, hold and see
one leaf for half an hour until you loved it,
instead of pushing on to better, best?

I am holding a leaf, now, about a hundred
years later, and I see it is every bit as good
as any leaf ever was. Even the ones before
you lived, Mother, before it all went downhill.
I am crying holding you and me, for we are good.

Territories

From Land's End,
up on Sutro's ruined observatory,
we gaze along the dwindling shore.
The air is empty, mild, and gray,
the wind away, the tide low
and the sea, for once, silent.

For us too a quiet moment, Sister.
You here from the East,
Ativan-calmed, fears of getting lost
forever on route, of finding me
the Devil, fearfully left behind,
normal abnormal self left behind.

Your world turns on a new axis
in a place far west of you
and it is me and what is mine,
a temporary stasis you want
to last forever. But I
cannot promise that even to myself.

Suddenly, a redtailed hawk

and a crow, large

though still half his size,

materialize and swoop up

the cliff face, wheeling

belly to belly in widening spirals,

hawk screaming,

shadow-black crow cawing,

each fury paralleling

the other's flight precisely:

to defy and chase away?

or invite for play?

Above the Golden Gate, Blue Angels

chew through sky in the same ventral formation

to thrill Fleet Week crowds,

mirroring each other with no more precision

and far less grace than our living birds,

though cast matching from the same metal.

The birds sunder and fall

and the jets claim your attention:

Wowie! Lookit! you croon,

your arm stuck straight out,

a beacon for the warplanes

turning with a ravening sound.

Family Dog

You, poor Shelty, became neurotic,
driven as much by the need to keep us
together as we by the need to burst apart.

The closeness you craved we hated,
wild for freedom from each other—
the quiet peace of separate ice floes.

While we split and screamed
across rooms or fled to hideouts,
you ran yelping to and fro, herding

and herding your frantic flock
who could not guide themselves or
let you—or anyone—take charge.

You were like a stymied tightrope walker
balanced only because drawn equally
to the abyss on both sides.

So you extended your obsession to cars,

nipping at their tires as at our ankles,

hopelessly trying to shepherd them

as you tried to make us a family

bound by anything but pain. Struck,

you nearly died for trying.

Quadriplegic, incontinent, whimpering all

day and night, you shocked us all by

living, walking, then running (stiffly) again—

only because the one least likely, sister schiz,

herself damaged and radiant with helpless hurt,

found a healing power and let it out.

She danced with rage and howled

when we said you should be put away:

 "No, let me help him, let me!"

Hand-feeding, sleeping touching you always

(the only way to stop your constant wailing),

she lived in the stink of your piss and crap.

I, hauling out sodden newspapers (the *least*

you can do, they said), wished you dead

and me free: belief in Nothing froze away

my pain and left me bright as a winter tree,

as if, so often wished, she too were put away,

and the whole empty world simply mine.

But she won—made you stay alive for weeks

until you knew there was no choice but mend.

Perhaps it was her way to pay for that kitten

she'd hit and innocently killed years before,

enraged because it would not purr for her.

Or perhaps because she could not cure herself

she poured her unused store of healing

into you, who lived years more, still

faithfully herding us and the straying cars.

Later, when her voices reviled her,

she could answer that at least she'd saved you,

given you every new mouthful of joy.

And when my brightness turned dark,

I could remember that hope and light

survive in the most astonishing places.

Elegy (in Advance) for My Sister

I wonder what you might have been
given a different set of planets
at your birth, a kinder God
Or much better luck.

There's no knowing what
you could have done in good time:
written some unforgettable poem,
made or played music so fine

that all those who now back away
with quick embarrassed glances
might have hung entranced
in orbit around your sun.

None of this happened.
You were born wrong, stunted early,
and became a remote, dark planet,
a bit of ice on the outer edge

of the mind's known universe.
I have tried to warm you,
to send a spark of light into
your ongoing night,

but I am inhabited by heat-
loving spirits and cannot
venture as far—my orbit circling
closer to our sane strong star

even at my miserable apogee—
as your far-flung ellipse
has wandered. Only
in the end, if a supernova

at the source
of both our beings
consumes my hurtling nearness instantly
but lets you linger

in your suddenly warming space
perhaps a moment,
will you know how good it is
to be warm and bright,

admired and caressed by light.
Before the hurricane of flame
burns you to black ash and gas,
you will know I loved you.

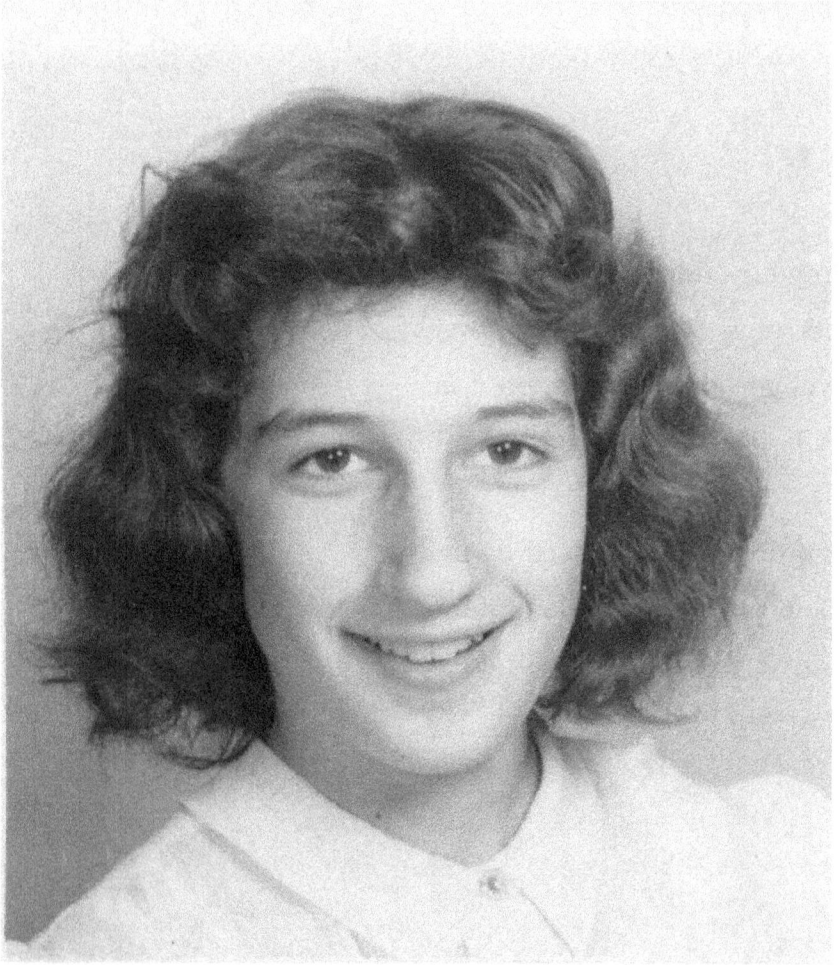

Step-Sister at Sixteen and After

Such a sound and social animal,
eager for the doorbell or the phone,
you wanted least of all to be alone
which I wanted only, or to be with you.
But you never welcomed me,
morose and inward male,
child of Mother's second marriage
you were told to love.

Your antipathy was legend:
spilled me from my bassinet;
left me for lost in Sears
climbing the down escalator
up to you; would not come
when a punk in black
tripped me at the skating rink
and I gashed my chin and bled.

It's nothing, you snapped,
stop that baby bawling!
I let you have ten minutes' more
screaming, but now I understand:

Why should you care for me and not
sail on in tights and pompoms,
the swan who captured every eye
till the little bastard burst your dream.

He stole your mother and now he wanted *you*.
No! Saved for the tall tough guy in black.
Ten years later, you got him, all of him:
the thrill of casual cruelty, tears,
the make-up embrace, guilt's sweet bite.
Half a century later, two children grown
and gone, you've held out and hardened
as his tallness and his toughness wore down.

But I bet your mind replays sometimes
that frigid day Buddy Holly crashed in snow
and you sobbed, *God why did he go*?
I didn't get why anyone would care
about some rock-and-roll idol shaken
from a distant sky, but I almost
took your hand and said *there, there.*
Almost.

Did you lose your one true love that day?
Did something inside you tear away,
some innocence shear off to leave a pain
you could never soothe—only abuse
or love? I hold your wedding photo:
the man in black behind, not touching;
you, lace white, face bright,
gazing dreamily toward the frame.

If it wasn't Buddy you missed, then who?
The father you barely knew,
shot from the wartime sky
before you were five?
You were a virgin when you wed
(I found the "how to" manual by your bed),
a Fifties girl who saved it for marriage,
and even now I think of you as

virginal, full of emptiness and hope,
saving something precious
for that special one who'll never come
or came and went. I want to go to you,

say *there, there*, put my arm around you
and glide across the ice side by side,
like planes rising beyond the frame—
till that man in black knifes in, and I fall away.

Aunt Lottie

In the photo you perk
with barely contained mirth,
your *OK wiseguy I'm on to you* look
caught in the angle of your head,
mouth up on one side,
eyes narrowed, appraising,
but glinting at the corners.

A landsman, you cried
at an L.A. Sears, grinning
hugely as you and some salesman
you knew not from Moses launched
into nonstop Yiddish, and suddenly
there was the past I was missing,

second-generation, homogenized Jew,
the identity I told my shrink
I lacked—not American, not Jewish,
nothing but totally inadequate—

it was in the language, eppes,

the language! The cradle in which I

might have been rocking if

my parents, so desperate to keep it

a secret (shame?) had shared

the only wealth they would ever have.

At last, after hoking for half an hour

about all the mishpocheh including this

wonderful nephew Herr Professor

you bought the damned refrigerator.

And when you were mugged outside the bank

by the farshtinkener shvartzer, hoo boy!

you said, I gave as good as I got, some joy.

Always some joy, eating or talking or

pounding your broom on the ceiling,

screaming Formach dein pisk! My nephew the Professor

is sleeping, shut up, Russian shtunk!

Always some joy, even when your husband,

Jack the clothier, dropped dead.

He was always in a hurry,

it's no exception, you laughed as you cried.

Years later, we shopped for blouses—I, my shiksa wife

and you, grown huge by then, chuckling slyly,

my bosoms are my best point, you know,

I gotta show them off. Yes, Lottie, the shiksa said,

but you can't wear size 9 any more

or you'll show them more than that!

And you grinned, as you might have grinned

after you broke your arm in the bathroom,

between shouts for help, as the rest of your mind

gave way and you tumbled from that tub into

dementia. Still, you tried your OK wiseguy look

while yelling in the nursing home, this guy

is not my nephew he's a gonif after my money,

and I never figured out if you believed it,

but you grinned after they put the catheter in—

how wonderful not to have to shlep to the pot.

And blissfully peed as you lay there, beaming.

The phone rang at 2 AM. It's bad,

a resistant infection, your doctor said.

She's going down fast. Should I write a no-code?

What's that?

We let her go.

This might sound crazy, Doctor,

but is she smiling?

Smiling?

Veh iz mir!

She wouldn't

remember how.

Eppes, a landsman

I thought.

Then please, Doctor,

let her go.

Hear, O Israel

Out in the fog, voices
too soft to comprehend
argue mildly; feelings too mixed
to untangle fly crisscross
like toy arrows.
Car doors slam, the hoarse bark
of a starter motor becomes more shrill
until its parent engine roars
to life and carries this configuration
out of sound and sight.

Alone again in my study,
myself and the mist to listen to,
I long to be in that car and hear
all that rode away:
who did wrong, who right,
what squabble lost or won,
who rewarded, who punished—

all those sodden dramas
that make up family life,
sour as old sweat,
snug as a bedbug.

That was a time when loneliness
always had company and boredom
was brightened by the next scheme.
No need to find meaning then,
to make a life of my own,
for we were tied together as one
and that was our meaning thus far:
to be carried by the family car
in the labyrinth of family roads
as long as needed to keep us there.

Uncle Jack

A small man,

clothes-pole thin,

you believed everything

should be perfect:

manicured your nails each week,

slicked down your hair Fifties style

and sported a gold watch

(five hunnerd dollars! you crowed),

jackets socks ties all silk

and in the black billfold

thick wads of dough.

God's gift to women

Mother groaned.

I was awestruck.

You did magic tricks

with a silver dollar,

shook my hand

as if I were a man,

gave me nickels, gold-

wrapped chocolate coins

and cowboy shirts from L.A.,

taught me to tie a windsor knot

and laughed a loud bark

when finally I got it.

But even a nine-year old

(especially this nine-year old)

could feel the dark river

rippling through you,

cold waters from which

a white mist rose

to blank your face

as you looked away.

Polishing yourself

like your Chevy

to a perfect shine

just in time for the rain,

you merely postponed the dirt

I knew waited, no matter how

clean the nails

tan the skin

bright the smile

gold the watch.

Death would snap you in two

like a stringbean crisp with morning dew.

Aunt Lottie knew this

when with every smile she leaned close,

loving you so much more, Jack

than you could ever love her back.

Was I a prescient or merely morbid child?

I don't know, but as you walked

in downtown Los Angeles

one sunny afternoon

your heart exploded.

A miracle that no one took
the watch the wallet the cash.

They left all that, your legacy,
as you lay perfectly flat,
like a chocolates box
gift-wrapped but empty.

Left the trim
but took poor Jack,
took God's gift back.

Aunt Frances

The only picture left of you
was snapped by my four-year-old mind.
The print has faded, the negative's lost,
this great remove from you alive.

I recall a face of ardent beauty, white
and smooth, fragrant like a flower,
a tapered artist's hand drawing faces
in the sand, your grown body magically
shrinking to fit beside mine in the toy
Model T you gave me, tiny fairy
with your fairy child. Brown hair windblown,
green eyes sparkling, slender fingers curled
around my own, you slammed the stickshift home.
A bulb would squeeze to make a real horn sound
as we laughed and laughed and I drove fast
while the whole world spun by, powering
up the high path in the park, skidding
over the bare dirt on the ridge, driving down
into our private glen, thick with grass,
crunchy leaves, the sweet-sour smell of Fall.

Then you were gone, purged from the photos
as if you'd never been. Dead, Mother said.
Gone away, like Eddie the spaniel, remember?

I climbed high up a sticky pine tree
to find where on earth you might be
and the wild sky pulled at me like a kite.
I could soar after you on the lifting wind
but then, like a stone, I'd smash down again,
and be gone too. So I clung sobbing to the rocking
branch till Dad told me where to put my feet.

Down, I drove every patch
of our glen: squirrels snickered,
glossy crows cawed, mad at me,
but you weren't there.

Hiding in the trees?
Yes, but you wouldn't come out.

Next time?

Our last picnic before winter

I left the Model T on the trail,

no longer wanting to miss you.

Then I made us go back to find it.

Too late.

You'd gotten in

and driven away.

Poet Shows Young Nephew
the High Sierra

Truly, it was a tarn,

a word nearly as lovely

as the banked Alpine hills

around bluedark waters

deepening the sky, the trees

more piercingly rooted,

much more steep,

crownside down

than trunkside up.

You were skipping young

across the felled pines, leaping

astonishing distances rock

to rock

as if you knew no weight,

no care for the water,

icecold, sinking below.

You gave a wild wave,

shouted come on old man!

laughed as the echoes died.

Not yet, I muttered, not old yet
but at the first long gap
hips locked tight,
thighs gave way,
and I was alone
with my reflections,
the only world where I
could still leap agile,
thought to thought.

The depth of that tarn
dwelt more luminous live
than any shifting or rooted
upper world: jays flashing,
clouds shaping,
trees impeccably upright,
sky filling the shores,
each caught and held
undiminished in depth
long after upper
passing.

There you were again—
suddenly as if risen
from the actual water
or landed from the sky—
your face, your trunk
beside mine in both worlds.

This is so cool, I love this,
you and yourself blurted out.
Yes, I said, have you noticed
how much more vivid the reflected
world is than the real one?
You could live and die in there.

Sure, Uncle Dan, and fish can fly
up here, but what I want to know is
where can we get a good cheeseburger?

Mother

1

In primordial time I
four years old found
amid sodsmelling grass
a tan stick, manmade,
swirled black pattern
luminous, portending,
as you walked beside
to chocolate icecreamland
through a sunwarmed field.

It's a fountain pen, you said
to write on paper with,
bought a squat bottle,
levered up black ink, and scribed
a magic line direct from mind
to dancing hand.
Let me, I shouted, wanting only
to curl that script out of myself.

Imagine a cat lies quiet, you said,

dozing on this line across the paper,

purring, dreaming of icecream dinner

till a mouse wakes up and leaves its house,

trotting by, and pussy so surprised scrambles

up to chase! White hand-cat swept across

a snowfield, leaving black-ink tracks.

Follow the kitty chasing the mousie,

see how they run, that's how it's done.

2

Years later I mastered the magic letters

and used them to write thoughts,

not mine but Americanism essays (good

training for life, you said), won silver

dollars, more allowance, but all seemed

undeserved, as if you'd put those sentences

in my mind (did I *care* about America?)

as now you spent your waking time

telling disturbed children how to think their lives.

In ninth grade, you taught me how to type
and think as I typed, so in one draft
I finished what took other kids three.
I moved inward as you moved away,
and, silent, thought and wrote my life
as yours sank with your psychotic daughter
who could never get enough of anyone,
so hurt was she and so deprived.
I was left with dreams and words.

Graduated at last, I got my own sweet cat,
liquid black arc shearing through day,
rippling through night, alert even at rest,
knowing truths I would never know,
walking away just as I thought she would stay.
Once she caught a mouse, ate it head first, twitching
tail disappearing last. Crunch. You were gone,
swallowed up by daughter misery.

3

The year your cancer found you,

caught you in its hard embrace,

I got no silver prize, but found paper money

everywhere: on sidewalks, washed ashore

on ocean waves, on the college stairway,

second step—a hundred dollars or more. Hush

money? A wink and a nod, not to complain?

How could I take something for nothing, you eaten away?

Beside the hospital door, a bush held out another fiver.

That was our last visit.

Lying on your back, still, your belly

swollen with death, you said

I seem to have lost my eyesight.

(Her kidneys have failed, the whitecoat

whispered.) It's alright Ma, I'm here.

I took your hand. You did not clasp back,

for you had already left that hand,

as long ago you'd left my life.

I thought I had more years to give,

you spoke again. To help those kids.

(Help *her*, though you didn't say it.)

I love you Ma, I said, but perhaps

you couldn't hear either, or respond.

I left late that afternoon as the autumn sun,

punctured, sank, and bloodied a cloudy sky.

Left, my five-dollar bill, your silence, and I.

By dawn you were dead.

4

During the service Dad said

he saw you hovering above,

against the faux-church ceiling

of the reform temple, buoyed

by organ music. Funny, he said,

how the mind makes a mirage from dire

need: I know it's an illusion but I still

see her there like a cloud. (I saw nothing

but him seeing, unbelieving.)

They weren't really ashes, more

granules or nuggets, but white

like pumice or calcined popcorn

stored in a canister like a candy tin,

thin goldcoated metal

housing those last few cups of you.

We stumbled through Zoar Valley,

startling sparrows coming home to rest,

until the trail stopped at a precipice.

Staring at a hillside leafed gold and red,

Oh it's beautiful, she'll love it here!

your damaged daughter said, so we took

a handful each and flung it from the cliff. You fell

into the downslope dirt, shy of the brilliance beyond.

I threw fistfuls, straining colorward,

but all my might fell short, until your daughter

shrieked, let me, she's mine too, grabbed,

and spun the scattering canister from my hand.

5

Just as in life, there was not enough,
could never be enough of you.
We squabbled like a litter over the bones
of your bones, rending your peace even
in that peaceable valley. How you must have
hated us both as we fed on your attention,
like that cancer on your flesh, always wanting—
but your hate could not face itself and changed to duty
with the name of love: *I must, you must, we must, love.*

Tumbling down the cliff, gold against the blue-cold
autumn sky and then the gray rock, your last home
spilled the last of you. Our accusations were your only
prayers: Look what you made me do! We could not share
your death as neither could get share enough in life.
Were we *both* unnatural, I more sane (or sly) than she,
or were you simply not meant to be a mother, struggling
to be free, to chew loose, hide, and, private, bleed,
in the only way allowed, for another's wounded child?

Oh, for crying out loud! Dad shouted,
throwing his hands wide as if this last scene
trumped all others, sealed the sullen
package of his life. Turning up his face, he
searched the sky, and finding nothing,
turned and labored up the path. What a waste,
he muttered, she'll never know she's here,
in this lovely place. Dark congealed around us, each,
as we drove, through thickening twilight, back home.

6

The next month I began to write,
my dissertation, then the story of my life
(the gift, or penalty, of yours). Thoughts struck
quick from my mind, words catpawed across
the page and sleeked down on their prey:
no fleeing mouse could get away. In your dresser
was a story written young, when you still dreamed:
a woman dying, unfulfilled, in crisp hospital sheets—
White on White, the title. The death, your own, foretold?

As I wrote, some echo of you came and curled in me,
as if the floating ghost from the Temple or that anchored
apparition daughter-sister saw a week later,
sitting in her bedroom chair, had wandered, orphan,
into me, cold, exposed, seeking shelter from the fleshless
air. You built a slow and kindly fire to burn within me
and mourned that only dead could you come near
approving me, not blaming for wanting too much or too
little. This time, *I carried you* and gave you birth again.

Written out, I went back to selling my time and you
receded. As if I'd nursed you, watched you grow and break
away, I knew you'd come back when you wanted, free now
to be, no ligatures of living holding you from me.
At winter's end, one raw morning I found my cat smashed
dead on the road. But the first warm spring night she sat
on the windowsill more alive than ever. I believed, and
when she leapt down and blended with the night, I knew
she would return, like the moon, when the time was right.

Suicide (Aunt Frances)

She fell in beauty always
falling
from sky to
sky

lovely along the treetops
shimmering with
wind
the poplars' veins
fine against the
gray

In mind always she never
struck
and roots of hair
downseeking soil
found only
air

a momentary aerophyte

she

in beauty always

falling

Mother Loss

They were huge old elm trees,
and on the ground softly were
their sour leaves, rotting red to brown
in raw November rain.

I remember you wore
wonderfully that day
a tweed suit, blue-brown,
jacket framing a red-gold scarf.

I looked down at you
from my height, shy secret son,
and felt the keen of time's bright
blade slice between us.

I remember thinking, some day
I will look back and remember
this day, this day I first knew,
deeply, you would be gone.

Your fragility opened in me then,
sweet flower of pain, before I knew my own.
Your glance of guarded affection
was always uncertain, holding back

some large part as if embarrassed
or protecting me from what
I came to know in that moment:
love is too huge

ever to grasp or hold,
to contain or be contained,
in anyone beloved—it is too vast
and we are too small and passing.

I looked into your eyes
those thirty brief long years ago
and saw the pain of spring ice
almost warm enough to melt—

but we were very deep in Fall.
And you looked back within me
and said nothing, saying everything:
that you would go and I would go

and each of us would hold and be held
only by this moment, *this moment*
when we both lived at last
what small love we could, restrained

by an icy skim of pain: the larger love,
smiling far off, beneath, beyond,
neither of us could ever say
on this or any other living day.

Yom Kippur Dialogue

I found myself sitting, looking
at a photo album of my family,
and wondered what the hell for.
They're all dead, a voice said,
and you can't do anything about it.

Another answered, yes you can:
remember them, make your mind
a womb in which they gestate
and are born again.

I looked out at the world and saw
it was all turning away,
and a voice said, so it goes—
and you can't do
a damned thing about it.

but another said, oh yes you can:
paint it, paint it rich and fine
so all of us remember
to live again.

In a Catholic Church

Are all these steady flames,
like luminescence in a calm sea,
really souls or signs of souls?
As the warm wax hardens,
so does my mind
that wants everything
but believes nothing.

Lacking a God,
I've borrowed someone else's,
but burning this candle for my dead
is treacherous comfort
because the flame can't possibly
warm or light them home.
And because it might.

You who are gone—
Father? Mother?

Is it my fault you left me
only your deaths?

The Tooth Fairy's quarter
clinks in the almsbox:
how right that I return it,
I, who never believed.

The tooth was gone for good,
and I knew no coin could buy it back:
my tongue proved the gap
empty as the poor Fairy
(delicate and tattered as a cloud).

When Tinkerbell was dying
for love of Peter Pan
and each child had a duty
to wish her back again,
I watched her silver blood dim
and knew she'd die because of me,
the one boy who would not believe.

Father! Mother!
I longed for her to live
as I long for you.

But you followed her
to Neverneverland,
and left me coin
that cannot buy you back
and faith in nothing.

This candle's tears
draw out my own.
It burns as much for me
as you.

Kol Nidre in Driftwood for Mother

What have you to say to me,
you who have come so far
over the salt road of the sea?

Would you tell me, as she did,
all my miseries are nothing
to yours, swelling in that twisting sun?

I remember her at the end,
not quite so misshapen as you,
but close, close, and tortured

as fully by bright chemicals
as you by that merciless sun
until eyes failed, everything failed.

No matter how blinding the pain,
some vision must surely remain:
not the mere dark curtain?

I appear to have lost my sight
was all you said, as if rehearsing lines,
then groped for the exit and found

after a last flex of lung, the merciful

plunge from the proscenium

into rows of still bodies.

No applause for your final scene,

picking daisies from the sheet,

but a quiet awe of this deed—

finding white on white

beneath the sealing blanket of dark.

I had promised to stay with you but

let your hand slip between breaths.

I had promised to stay with you but

you slipped my hand between breaths.

I *have* stayed, say the still watchers.

And you, spirit seared into wood,

Come to tell me it is time to be free.

Born Again

Late in life, Dad,
several inches shrunken,
you slept curled on your side
like an ancient child,
sucking and smacking,
pale red lips pouted
at a teat of mere air—
yet, comforted,
you sighed and slipped
into stillness.

I wonder
when I am withered
to gnome size
and ready for the last comfort
who will watch me to sleep
as I mumble the dream nipple,
born again.

Dad

I dreamed of you
convivial in death
like the pal
I wanted you to be.
Like the pal perhaps
you wanted me to be.

This time
no monster-movie skull
shrieked from the back seat,
no clawing hand
gripped my shoulder
and the gnawing mink of fear
fed quietly in a corner.

Parallel on blankets,
soft as butter knives,
we chatted
amiably of this and that.
No rage or rough intent
serrated the edge between us.

Are we closer now
because you died
or because
someday I will?

I am not afraid.

141

Family Album

Trying to become more alive,
why do I dwell always
on my dead? Leaving,
did they take part of my life too,
so I ask them
give it back, give me back?
Or do I want what they
never could give me alive:
love and a blessing?
Am I a ghoul, rooting life
from the soil of their deaths
as a pig digs truffles?
Are they the ghouls,
hungry for my living flesh
to cover their naked bones?
Would they have me dead, too,
to salve their loneliness
or do I call them to life
to save me from mine?
Can we be alive *and* dead?

These flat photographs,
no more living than the
paper they are printed on
yet wrench at me, sing
songs to me, long for me,
so goddamned abandoned
by all time, so compressed
by all space to small square cells
within blank white bars.

Mother, Father: you, departed.
Sisters: you, lost in life.
All you others, living and dead—
I can only remember and weep
and hope the tears are not so salty
they stunt my roots that start in you,
not so wet they wash away your soil,
but warm and rich and buoyant
to lift you high into my veins,
and nourish all our lives in mine
that we may live together
the more we die apart.

www.ingramcontent.com/pod-product-compliance
Lightning Source LLC
Chambersburg PA
CBHW021154020426
42331CB00003B/51